T0353192

JOSH AZOUZ

Josh Azouz's plays include *Buggy Baby*, *The Mikvah Project*
(Yard Theatre); *10,000 Smarties* (Old Fire Station); *The Bike*
(Royal Court in Pimlico Playground). He has been selected for
writers' groups at the Royal Court, the Bush, and been on
attachment at the National Theatre Studio. Theatre directing
credits include *The Man Who Almost Killed Himself* (Edinburgh
Fringe/BBC iPlayer/Odeon cinemas); *Come in Sit Down*
(Tricycle Theatre); He co-created *Sink or Shpin,* the world's
first comedy show with an audience on exercise bikes. Josh is
an associate artist for The Yard and MUJU (a Muslim-Jewish
theatre company).

Other Titles in this Series

Josh Azouz
BUGGY BABY &
    THE MIKVAH PROJECT

Mike Bartlett
ALBION
BULL
GAME
AN INTERVENTION
KING CHARLES III
WILD

Tom Basden
THE CROCODILE
HOLES
JOSEPH K
THERE IS A WAR

Jez Butterworth
THE FERRYMAN
JERUSALEM
JEZ BUTTERWORTH PLAYS: ONE
MOJO
THE NIGHT HERON
PARLOUR SONG
THE RIVER
THE WINTERLING

Elinor Cook
THE GIRL'S GUIDE TO SAVING
    THE WORLD
IMAGE OF AN UNKNOWN
    YOUNG WOMAN
THE LADY FROM THE SEA
    after Ibsen
PILGRIMS

Vivienne Franzmann
BODIES
MOGADISHU
PESTS
THE WITNESS

James Fritz
COMMENT IS FREE
    & START SWIMMING
THE FALL
LAVA
PARLIAMENT SQUARE
ROSS & RACHEL

Stacey Gregg
LAGAN
OVERRIDE
PERVE
SCORCH
SHIBBOLETH
WHEN COWS GO BOOM

Ella Hickson
THE AUTHORISED KATE BANE
BOYS
EIGHT
ELLA HICKSON PLAYS: ONE
OIL
PRECIOUS LITTLE TALENT
    & HOT MESS
WENDY & PETER PAN *after* Barrie
THE WRITER

Vicky Jones
THE ONE
TOUCH

Anna Jordan
CHICKEN SHOP
FREAK
POP MUSIC
THE UNRETURNING
YEN

Arinzé Kene
GOD'S PROPERTY
GOOD DOG
LITTLE BABY JESUS
MISTY

Lucy Kirkwood
BEAUTY AND THE BEAST
    with Katie Mitchell
BLOODY WIMMIN
THE CHILDREN
CHIMERICA
HEDDA *after* Ibsen
IT FELT EMPTY WHEN THE
    HEART WENT AT FIRST BUT
    IT IS ALRIGHT NOW
MOSQUITOES
NSFW
TINDERBOX

Evan Placey
CONSENSUAL
GIRLS LIKE THAT
GIRLS LIKE THAT & OTHER PLAYS
    FOR TEENAGERS
JEKYLL & HYDE *after* R.L. Stevenson
PRONOUN

Stef Smith
GIRL IN THE MACHINE
HUMAN ANIMALS
REMOTE
SWALLOW

Sam Steiner
KANYE THE FIRST
LEMONS LEMONS LEMONS
    LEMONS LEMONS

Jack Thorne
2ND MAY 1997
BUNNY
BURYING YOUR BROTHER IN
    THE PAVEMENT
A CHRISTMAS CAROL *after* Dickens
HOPE
JACK THORNE PLAYS: ONE
JUNKYARD
LET THE RIGHT ONE IN
    after John Ajvide Lindqvist
MYDIDAE
THE SOLID LIFE OF SUGAR WATER
STACY & FANNY AND FAGGOT
WHEN YOU CURE ME
WOYZECK *after* Büchner

Phoebe Waller-Bridge
FLEABAG

Elliot Warren
FLESH AND BONE

Josh Azouz

VICTORIA'S KNICKERS

*Lyrics by Josh Azouz, Chris Cookson and
members of the National Youth Theatre*

NICK HERN BOOKS

London

www.nickhernbooks.co.uk

A Nick Hern Book

Victoria's Knickers first published in Great Britain in 2018 as a paperback original by Nick Hern Books Limited, The Glasshouse, 49a Goldhawk Road, London W12 8QP

Victoria's Knickers copyright © 2018 Josh Azouz
Lyrics copyright © Josh Azouz, Chris Cookson and members of the National Youth Theatre

Josh Azouz has asserted his moral right to be identified as the author of this work

Cover Photography by Mark Cocksedge

Designed and typeset by Nick Hern Books, London
Printed in the UK by Mimeo Ltd, Huntingdon, Cambridgeshire PE29 6XX

A CIP catalogue record for this book is available from the British Library

ISBN 978 1 84842 816 4

CAUTION   All rights whatsoever in this play are strictly reserved. Requests to reproduce the texts in whole or in part should be addressed to the publisher.

Amateur Performing Rights   Applications for performance, including readings and excerpts, by amateurs in the English language throughout the world should be addressed to the Performing Rights Manager, Nick Hern Books, The Glasshouse, 49a Goldhawk Road, London W12 8QP, *tel* +44 (0)20 8749 4953, *email* rights@nickhernbooks.co.uk, except as follows:

Australia: Dominie Drama, 8 Cross Street, Brookvale 2100, *tel* (2) 9938 8686, *fax* (2) 9938 8695, *email* drama@dominie.com.au

New Zealand: Play Bureau, PO Box 9013, St Clair, Dunedin 9047, *tel* (3) 455 9959, *email* info@playbureau.com

United States of America and Canada: United Agents, see details below

Professional Performing Rights   Applications for performance by professionals in any medium and in any language throughout the world should be addressed to United Agents, 12–26 Lexington Street, London W1F 0LE, *tel* +44 (0)20 3214 0800, *fax* +44 (0)20 3214 0801, *email* info@unitedagents.co.uk

No performance of any kind may be given unless a licence has been obtained. Applications should be made before rehearsals begin. Publication of this play does not necessarily indicate its availability for amateur performance.

Woodland
CARBON
www.woodlandcarbon.co.uk
NICK HERN BOOKS
Printed on Carbon Captured paper

Victoria's Knickers was first performed by the National Youth
Theatre of Great Britain at Soho Theatre, London, on
27 October 2018. The cast was as follows:

LAURIE	Laurie Ogden
ISABEL	Isabel Adomakoh Young
ED	Jamie Ankrah
VICTORIA	Alice Vilanculo
DUCHESS	Simran Hunjun
GARY	Jeffrey Sangalang
CONROY	Muhammad Abubakar Khan
LEN	Christopher Williams
ALBERT	Oseloka Obi
ERNST	Jay Mailer
BRUNHILDA	Olivia Dowd
LEAH	Leah Mains
FRED	Fred Hughes-Stanton
REFEREE	Marilyn Nnadebe
SONIA	Olivia Dowd
DR FEEL GOOD	Jay Mailer
THE FISHERMAN	Jeffrey Sangalang
REVELLER	Jay Mailer
SASHA	Aidan Cheng
CECIL	Olivia Dowd
OFFICER TROY	Fred Hughes-Stanton
TONI	Francesca Regis
MUSICIANS	Kazuma Costello
	Natalie Smith
	Isabelle Stone
Writer	Josh Azouz
Director	Ned Bennett
Composer	Chris Cookson
Lyrics	Josh Azouz, Chris Cookson and
	members of the National Youth
	Theatre

Designer	Hannah Wolfe
Lighting Designer	Jess Bernberg
Sound Designer	Giles Thomas
Music Producer	Jason Elliot
Musical Director	Arlene McNaught
Bryan Forbes *Assistant Director*	Meghan Doyle
Assistant Designer	Sally Hardcastle
Associate Sound Designer	Esme Lewis-Gartside
Production Manager	Ian Smith
Production Sound	Hope Brennan
Company Stage Manager	Dougie Wilson
Deputy Stage Manager	Ruth Collett
Assistant Stage Managers	Tom Beaumont
	Phoebe Francis
Head of Costume	Helena Bonner
Deputy Head of Costume	Elia Baker
Deputy Head of Wardrobe	Caitlin Shephard
Costume Members	Bianca Wilson
	Amy Yeates
Stage Management Members	Rohan Carr
	Sussan Sanii
	Molly Taylor
	Helena Fullman

national®
youth
theatre

The National Youth Theatre of Great Britain (NYT) is a world-leading youth arts organisation. NYT were established in 1956 as the first youth theatre in the world and have performed critically acclaimed productions over the past fifty-nine years. 2016 will be a celebration of their sixtieth year.

NYT's training is unique because they believe that the best place for young performers to learn is on stage in front of an audience. NYT showcase young talent on West End stages, in stadiums worldwide and at iconic sites both at home and abroad. They commission brave and relevant new writing and reinterpret classic stories for our time. They are as ambitious as the young people they serve.

NYT's world renowned alumni include: Helen Mirren, Daniel Craig, Chiwetel Ejiofor, Colin Firth, Rosamund Pike, Daniel Day-Lewis, Orlando Bloom, Catherine Tate, Ben Kingsley, Ashley Jensen, Derek Jacobi, Timothy Dalton, Zawe Ashton, Matt Lucas, Hugh Bonneville, Matt Smith and many more.

For more information visit **www.nyt.org.uk**

Acknowledgements

Victoria's Knickers was first developed with members of the NYT Epic Stages course in 2017. They are: Ciara Aaron, Samuel Armfield, Jaden Baker, Colm Bateman, Felicity Burgis, Edward Christensen, Kaz Costello, Katie Dolling, Sean Dougall, Hannah Dunlop, Oakley Flanagan, Jessica Friend, Naomi Gardener, Tiwalade Ibirogba Olulode, Minjeong Kim, Aruneema Lahon, Anna Mackay, Dominic McGovern, Charlotte-May Messer, Robert Meyer, Tiwai Muza, Sussan Sanii, Sebastian Schub, Ellie Smit, Natalie Smith, Nikoletta Soumelidis, Alice Vilanculo, Andrew White, Nathan Whitebrook, Ramon Wilson.

I'd like to thank the NYT Epic Stages course participants 2017 and NYT REP Company 2018 for allowing me to draw on their imaginations.

Thank you to Ned Bennett for all his help in developing this story.

J.A.

Production Note

The original production of *Victoria's Knickers* was staged with minimal props and on a bare stage. This is very effective. However, directors and designers could also go to town.

If an interval is required it should be taken between 3.4 and 3.5.

Characters are not gender specific.

Characters

LAURIE	REFEREE
ISABEL	SONIA
ED 'THE BOY' JONES	DENNIS
VICTORIA	NORZGARD
DUCHESS	DR FEEL GOOD
GARY	FISHERMAN
CONROY	TRACEY
LEN	REVELLER
ALBERT	SASHA
ERNST	CECIL
BRUNHILDA	OFFICER TROY
LEAH	TONI
FRED	

Note on Text

Words in brackets ( ) should be played by the actor, not said out loud.

…indicates a hesitation, unspoken or unfinished thought, or when a character is searching for a word.

A forward slash (/) indicates the point at which the next speaker interrupts.

This text went to press before the end of rehearsals and so may differ slightly from the play as performed.

1.1

1838. London.

ED JONES *is up a tree. He's looking at Buckingham Palace.*

At the bottom of his tree sit LAURIE *and* ISABEL.

LAURIE (*to audience*). One evening outside Buckingham Palace. (*To* ISABEL.) Forget it, it's too risky.

ISABEL. What's the risk?

LAURIE. Trigger-happy guards bored out of their minds.

ISABEL. The guards aren't interested in a couple of kids, they just wanna keep their heads down, chat, do the crossword.

LAURIE. So we hop the wall via Ed's tree?

ISABEL. Then stroll across the lawn.

LAURIE. How do we get out?

ISABEL. The same way we got in.

LAURIE. They have dogs, you gonna be able to scale the wall with bloodhounds biting at your heels?

ISABEL. We'll be back over the wall before the dogs have left their kennels.

LAURIE. I say we just tag *this wall* and send a clear message to everyone / who

ISABEL. Forget some basic tag for tourists, we need to get inside, tag the manifesto and make the bitch read.

LAURIE. She needs to read one of my pamphlets.

ISABEL. I don't even read your pamphlets.

LAURIE. Yeah but you like colouring books.

ISABEL. Nobody reads them, they use them for roaches. So we're in the Palace –

LAURIE. Running away from armed guards and rabid dogs and what room do we even tag?

ISABEL. We head straight for her bedroom.

LAURIE. Girl's got two hundred and forty bedrooms.

ISABEL. Yeah but she'll have one main room she sleeps in.

LAURIE. Who knows she might literally sleep in a different bed every night.

ISABEL. Hang on, hang on.

LAURIE. We'll have to chat up a chambermaid, ask if the girl's got a favourite room?

ISABEL. Very good.

LAURIE. Pretend we work in the Palace otherwise the chambermaid will go apeshit.

ISABEL. What, disguise ourselves?

LAURIE. We'll have to.

ISABEL. Go to the laundry room first, pick out a costume, nice.

LAURIE. 'I'm a seamstress, it's my first day on the job, where's Her Majesty's chambers?'

ISABEL. Joker.

LAURIE. Okay let's do this I'm buzzing.

ISABEL *takes out two cans of spray paint.*

ISABEL. They'd run out of green.

LAURIE. Pink isn't our colour.

ISABEL. Who cares about the colour, it's the words that count!?

LAURIE. This is the biggest moment of our lives and for you to come out and say the colours don't count well I'm starting to lose all faith in you. Our manifestos have always been green, I'm not gonna risk martyring myself for pink.

ISABEL. '*Martyring*' what are you Joan of Arc?

LAURIE. Ed, do you feel comfortable tagging in pink?

ED. Not gonna lie your chat is so dead I zoned out.

ISABEL. Dickhead.

ED. To be fair it's been a long day.

ISABEL. Is it tiring work smoking opium?

ED. I didn't smoke. I was wrestling with a poem about the moon.

LAURIE. Let's hear it.

ED. It's bollocks, I couldn't figure out the form. Spent all afternoon walking up and down Waterloo Bridge.

ISABEL. Did you wank over the view for inspiration?

LAURIE. Why you gotta say something like that?

ISABEL. Just saying it how it is. Our brother is a / wanker –

LAURIE. Wanker.

LAURIE and ISABEL *snort.*

Through a window, ED *sees* VICTORIA.

A moment.

ED *lowers himself down on the Palace side of the wall, and disappears. His sisters are unaware.*

Seeing as we're at loggerheads with the colour choice, I say we abandon the tagging idea. Let's just try and actually find her. Talk her through the manifesto. She's our age, she'll probably be receptive.

ISABEL. What if she's not?

LAURIE. I brought this.

LAURIE *takes out a gun.*

Ed, what's the guard situation looking like?

Ed?

ISABEL. Typical. Old Flakey McFlakerson.

LAURIE. Unless he already went in?

ISABEL. Shit, do you think?

They climb the tree.

LAURIE. They *shot* Chartists in Newport.

ISABEL. Yeah but Welsh policeman are crazy.

LAURIE. I can't take another funeral.

ISABEL. Laurie, he'll be fine.

They disappear over the wall.

Inside Buckingham Palace.

The DUCHESS *enters and sits opposite* VICTORIA.

VICTORIA. I'm not hungry.

DUCHESS. Can I have an approximate time when you might be?

VICTORIA. We just ate.

DUCHESS. I saw you run to the bathroom after.

VICTORIA. I needed a shit.

DUCHESS. Good, the bowels are finally working. So glad we cut out dairy.

VICTORIA. I miss dairy.

DUCHESS. There's plenty of substitutes.

VICTORIA. What could ever truly replace ice cream, and don't say sorbet.

DUCHESS. Gary!

VICTORIA. *Mum.*

GARY *enters with a plate of hot food. Tries to feed*
VICTORIA. VICTORIA *keeps her mouth shut.*

DUCHESS. Don't you want to look beautiful on coronation
day?

VICTORIA....

DUCHESS. Do the horse.

GARY *makes a clip-clop sound and gallops a spoon towards*
VICTORIA*'s mouth.* VICTORIA *keeps it closed.*

GARY. Your Majesty you excited for Tuesday?

VICTORIA. Tuesday?

GARY. Prince Albert arrives.

VICTORIA. Oh yeah.

GARY. Everyone is talking about his eyes, dimples, apparently
he looks great in a vest –

DUCHESS. Thank you Gary.

GARY. Apologies Duchess.

CONROY *enters with just a towel around his waist. He's*
just come from the sauna.

CONROY. Wine.

GARY *brings* CONROY *a bottle of wine.* CONROY *chugs*
straight from the bottle.

When he's had enough he hands the bottle back to GARY.

Alright Vic.

VICTORIA. Yep.

CONROY. What are you thinking re: my appointment?

VICTORIA. I'm certainly considering it.

CONROY. If it's helpful I have the paperwork on my person.

VICTORIA. What?

CONROY. Or shall we just shake on it?

VICTORIA. Lord Conroy, I think it's best, if I wait till after the coronation before I um appoint my private secretary.

Beat.

CONROY. I could cry.

DUCHESS. She's not ready yet.

CONROY. Let me help her get ready.

DUCHESS. Why don't you general-manage the Palace instead?

CONROY. I'm not going to clean the fucking toilets.

DUCHESS. Course not, you're way beyond that. What about heading up security?

Beat.

That's settled then. (*To* VICTORIA.) 'Thank you, Mum.'

VICTORIA. Thank you, Mum.

DUCHESS. NOW EAT YOUR SUPPER!

VICTORIA opens her mouth. GARY feeds her.

Good girl.

This goes on for a while.

LAURIE and ISABEL enter along the back wall, unaware that they're walking through VICTORIA's dining room.

ISABEL. Perhaps we should just be tagging as we go?

LAURIE. No, we find Ed. Then we locate the virgin.

LAURIE and ISABEL suddenly become aware they're being watched.

They look at the ROYALS. The ROYALS look back.

Beat.

CONROY. GUARDS!

In what looks like a practised move, GARY rushes VICTORIA and DUCHESS offstage to safety.

LEAH! FRED!

LAURIE *sprays* CONROY*'s face.* ISABEL *whips off* CONROY*'s towel. Smirks.* ISABEL *and* LAURIE *run away.*

Guards LEAH *and* FRED *arrive.* CONROY *hides his manhood.*

Leah why are there two kids running around the Palace!?

LEAH. Lord Conroy, my team are on to them.

LEAH *and* FRED *run off.*

We hear gunshots.

CONROY, *now alone, looks at the audience.*

CONROY. Kids Chartists everyone needs to fucking burn.

CONROY *walks off.*

VICTORIA *is alone in her bedroom. She looks at the audience.*

Whistles. A string quartet run on.

VICTORIA (*singing*).
    Ordinary people, I am one of you,
    Inhibition lives in me too,
    I want to go and dance,
    Sip white wine with some girls,
    Ice-skate down the Thames at 4 a.m.

    Let me leave, this empty dream.
    Let me be, a people's Queen.

    Look at all the lights, let me get involved,
    Parties in dark places I don't know
    Chug a litre of tequila,
    Be cheeky with a stranger,
    Is that a spliff? Please give me one small toke.

    Let me leave, this empty dream.
    Let me be, a people's Queen.

1.2

In the Palace… later that night.

ED *is sat on the throne reading and munching on a lamb chop.*

ED *puts his book down and sings to us.*

ED (*singing*).
> I'm chilling on this throne,
> Among the green and the gold,
> And I like it. Brings out my eyes.
>
> There's a painting on the wall
> And he's checking me out
> I might kiss him. Just for kicks.
>
> Living my best life,
> Living my best life,
> Why
> Why did it take me so long?
> To be living my best life,
> Living my best life,
> Why
> Why did it take me so long?

VICTORIA *watches him, unnoticed.*

ED *takes a bite of his chop and then talks to us.*

Bruv these have been seasoned with something mad, I think it's jelly, getting currants up in here too OOOF. How you lot doing? Pretty jokes here, isn't it? For any of you who also live in shitholes I can't recommend this enough. Up sticks and find your nearest palace. Buckingham is my favourite. The interiors aren't entirely to my taste. Very minimal. I prefer a room with a clutter a room with history, but we'll soon sort that out.

VICTORIA *exits.*

(*Singing.*)
> This is where I'll live,
> Dine on foie gras and fizz,
> Make some memories. To tell all the kids.

No more pissing in the street,
Dealing drugs so I can eat
All that's over. Welcome to my home.

VICTORIA *enters with a massive rifle and edges slowly towards* ED.

Living my best life,
Living my best life,
Why
Why did it take me so long?
To be living my best life,
Living my best life,
Why
Why did it take me so –

VICTORIA *cocks her gun and presses it into the back of* ED*'s head.* ED *freezes.*

VICTORIA. You're sat on my throne.

ED. Steady on, coronation's five weeks away.

VICTORIA. I've been Queen for over a year.

ED. The King's been dead for over a year.

VICTORIA. You talking semantics!?

ED. I'm just not sure you're officially Queen until the Archbishop crowns you.

Beat.

VICTORIA *(re: the gun)*. You do realise this isn't a, telescope.

ED. Yeah, feels more like an Enfield Brunswick .704-calibre rifle.

VICTORIA. Shouldn't you be bricking it then!?

ED. Well it's a buzzkill. I don't wanna die. I've barely left a trace on the world. But this is your yard. If you wanna blow my brains out you'd be within your rights.

Beat.

VICTORIA. Turn around.

VICTORIA *keeps the gun aimed at* ED.

ED. Hello.

VICTORIA. Do you work in the kitchens?

ED. I'm an architect.

VICTORIA. Really, you look about twelve?

ED. Oh no I'm *legal*.

Beat.

I'm Ed by the way.

VICTORIA....

ED. And you are?

VICTORIA. Is that a joke?

ED. We've not really been introduced – felt rude to just come out with Victoria.

VICTORIA. Queen Victoria.

ED. Let's not start that one again.

VICTORIA. What are you doing on my throne!?

ED. Reading, bit of writing, very nearly masturbated.

VICTORIA. You trying to shock me?

ED. Just testing the waters.

VICTORIA. Well... the waters are very... icy... and full of sharks.

ED. I don't mean any harm, I've a good soul, honest.

VICTORIA. It's like some motherfucker's walked in from a Dickens novel.

ED. Hope not, I hate Dickens.

VICTORIA. Have you escaped from Bedlam?

ED. I'm from Kilburn boi.

VICTORIA. I'm not your boi.

Beat.

What are you doing in my home?

ED. Looking for somewhere to live.

VICTORIA. Well, as you can see, it's already occupied.

ED. What, all of it?

VICTORIA. Are you homeless?

ED. No I have a home. But I've outgrown it.

VICTORIA. Would you like me to get out the violins? They're on call twenty-four-seven.

Beat.

VICTORIA *lowers the gun.*

ED. It's very late to be up. Walking about. On your Jack Jones.

VICTORIA. I had a dream.

ED. I'm like Joseph when it comes to dreams.

VICTORIA *lets out a tiny smirk.*

ED*'s breathing shifts.*

'Waiting for You' instrumental starts.

VICTORIA. Some people think I'm too immature to handle the crown.

ED. Are you?

VICTORIA. I don't know.

ED. Just have to wait and see then.

VICTORIA. That's really… helpful… advice.

ED. I've always been good with advice. Although I'm a terrible listener. I get bored easily, need medication, but never found the right drugs.

VICTORIA. Keep trying.

ED. That's what my apothecary tells me.

> ED *looks down at his shoe.*

> I should have worn my other shoes. God I'd kill for some polish.

VICTORIA. The guards'll probably help you out with polish.

ED. You're not gonna call the guards we're chatting.

VICTORIA. They catch us *chatting*, you'll be thrown in jail.

ED. Chattin's a crime nowadays is it?

> *Beat.*

OFFSTAGE VOICE. VICTORIA!

> ED *retreats into the shadows.*

ED (*singing*).
> The best things in life are free my Queen. If you want to find out all you gotta do is follow me.

> VICTORIA *hides the gun.*

> DUCHESS *and* GARY *enter.*

DUCHESS. What are you doing out of bed!?

VICTORIA....sleepwalking.

> VICTORIA *walks around like she's possessed.*

DUCHESS. Don't lie to me.

> VICTORIA *stops and looks at her mother.*

1.3

A slum room in Kilburn. A tiny shithole of a place.

ISABEL *and* LEN *are looking in a long box.* LEN *is Welsh. In the corner sits* LAURIE, *very still.*

Pause.

LEN. Where do you get it?

ISABEL. My friend knows someone with connections in the international markets.

LEN. That sounds like bullshit.

ISABEL. Don't come into my home and tell me what's bullshit.

LEN. What's your friend's name?

ISABEL. What's with all the questions?

LEN. I like to know where things are from. How they were made.

ISABEL. No one was hurt in the making of this product.

Beat.

LEN. Let's talk price.

ISABEL. A pound?

LEN. You're having a laugh but.

ISABEL. A crown?

LEN. I'll go somewhere else.

ISABEL. What will you pay for it then?

LEN. Name me a price.

ISABEL. That's what I've just been doing.

LEN. Something sensible girl, I'm not a pudding.

Beat.

ISABEL. A shilling?

LEN. You kids are wasting my time, yer like uncle Huw at Christmas. I'll take this off your hands for a groat.

ISABEL. You're chatting breeze bruv.

LEN. I won't pay any more.

Beat.

LAURIE. Sod it – a groat.

ISABEL. Laurie!?

LAURIE. It's for the cause.

LEN *flicks* ISABEL *a coin.*

LEN. Onwards comrades the People's Charter marches forth.

Picks up the bag and exits.

ISABEL. Remind me not to take *you* to market.

LAURIE. You weren't negotiating you were just losing very slowly.

ED *enters.*

LAURIE *and* ISABEL *stare at* ED.

ED. Alright dickheads.

LAURIE. You've got some nerve.

A tense beat.

LAURIE *walks off.*

ED. What's up with her?

ISABEL. A Palace guard shot at her. Bullet came so close she heard the whistle.

ED. Is she hurt?

ISABEL. You disappeared!?

ED. We agreed a signal, not my fault if you're too / impatient.

ISABEL. We were supposed to be protesting together.

ED. You hurtin cos I wasn't gassed for your extra family day.

ISABEL. Go roadman on me and I'll break your fucking jaw.

ED.…

ISABEL. All these weeks… telling us you had their patrols
    down… that you'd be…

ED.…

ISABEL. Where did you go?

ED. Into the Palace.

ISABEL. Why didn't you wait for us?

ED. I'm writing a novel.

ISABEL. Jesus.

ED. No, it's about the monarchy. Sort of a romcom. There
    might be some torture.

ISABEL. Ed stop chatting shit for once in your life.

    Pause.

ED. I've met a girl.

ISABEL. Okay.

ED. I like her.

ISABEL. Good for you.

ED. Not sure if the feelings are mutual.

ISABEL. Was she giving out the signs?

ED. She pointed a gun at my face.

ISABEL. *Wait* who is she?

ED. You don't know her. To be honest I don't think you'd get
    on. You're very different people.

    Beat.

ISABEL. Where did you meet this girl?

ED. Just around.

ISABEL. When?

ED. I dunno.

Beat.

ISABEL. Go talk to Laurie. Apologise.

ED. She'll be smoking.

ISABEL. Ed.

Pause.

ED. How do you suss if someone's in to you?

ISABEL. ...

ED. I was hoping she might fiddle with her hair or something but there was none of that.

ISABEL. ...

ED. How do you *know*?

ISABEL. Everyone's different.

ED. Shit!

ISABEL. Calm down.

ED. Do you ever wish you could just hang out in someone else's brain?

ISABEL. Try showing her what you're about.

ED. What does that mean?

ISABEL. ...try to be open... so she might be. It's hard... I often play games, I hide – I think if I said this, if I told them I felt that... they'd be appalled.

(Too much information.) Show her where you're from. And hope she doesn't run.

Beat.

ED. In a bit.

ED *leaves.*

ISABEL *is alone.*

2.1

A copse in Windsor Gardens. There are fairy lights and lots of balloons.

ALBERT, ERNST *and* BRUNHILDA.

ALBERT (*in German*). This was a mistake.

ERNST (*in German*). Be cool Albert.

ALBERT (*in German*). We should have met in Buckingham Palace. I could have played her Chopin.

ERNST. Speak English.

ALBERT (*in German*). Why?

ERNST. Practice.

　[*When* ERNST *and* ALBERT *speak English there is no hint of an accent.*]

ALBERT. You prepare for something. You think about it at night. You wake up thinking about it. In the bath it goes round and around in your head. Practice practice practice and then the day approaches… I feel like a total wanker.

ERNST. Bro you're giving it a shot.

ALBERT. Who knows if she's even in to this music!?

ERNST. When she hears you sing, she's gonna melt.

ALBERT. Brunhilda.

BRUNHILDA. Albert.

ALBERT. From the top.

　BRUNHILDA *starts to play.*

　A tiny note comes out of ALBERT*'s mouth.*

　It's over. Take out your gun and shoot me.

ERNST. Can you just chill out!?

ALBERT. We might as well get the next boat home.

ERNST. They're coming.

ALBERT. Oh god!

> ERNST *stands next to* ALBERT *like he is best man at the wedding, moments before the bride enters.*

ERNST. Don't mention your shell collection.

ALBERT. Why not?

ERNST. Or that anecdote about a beetle.

ALBERT. On the boat you told me to be myself!?

ERNST. Yeah but you also need *game.* YOUR MAJESTY!

> VICTORIA, DUCHESS, CONROY *and* GARY *enter.*

DUCHESS. Call her cousin. We're all family here.

ERNST. Very well Aunt. Cousin Victoria. I'm Ernst. This is my little bro Albert.

VICTORIA. Hello. Cousins.

ERNST. Cousin Victoria do you like music?

VICTORIA. Yeah.

ERNST. Albert's prepared a song especially for you.

VICTORIA. Bit keen.

DUCHESS. Victoria!

ERNST. Get comfy and he'll start!

GARY. Your Majesty.

> GARY *gestures for where they should sit.*
>
> *The* ROYALS *sit.*
>
> ALBERT *sings a classical version of a contemporary pop song.*

On the second verse, ERNST *and* BRUNHILDA *join in.*

By the chorus, DUCHESS *and* CONROY *have joined in.*

At the end everyone is singing and looking at VICTORIA. VICTORIA *doesn't sing.*

The song is rising to its final chorus when LEN *walks into the copse, holding a sword.*

Everyone stops to look at LEN.

Silence.

LEN. I must say that is possibly the greatest rendition of that song I've ever heard. The harmonies. The gusto. Everyone getting stuck in giving it some welly. Except you Victoria. I see you. Holding back. Tapping your foot like a lemon. You also realise this singalong, this knees-up, is perverse. The fairy lights. The balloons. A party, a fucking party, whilst Newport is empty of fathers, husbands and sons.

LEN *pops all the balloons with his sword.*

Takes a moment to get his breath back.

The People's Charter want to love you but we're crying and bleeding for this vote. And we'll happily die for it. That's what you're up against. Thousands of people willing to die.

Say you'll think about it.

ALBERT. Brunhilda my fencing gear!

BRUNHILDA *rushes to get the fencing gear, then dresses* ALBERT.

Cousin Victoria I've been fencing competitively since the age of four. Didn't think I'd get the chance to show you so soon!

ALBERT, *now dressed to fight, strikes a pose.*

LEN *and* ALBERT *fight.*

LEN *has the upper hand but then chooses to stop fighting.*

Drops the sword.

Casually exits.

CONROY. LEAH! FRED!

LEAH *and* FRED *run on.*

LEAH. Lord Conroy, there's a Chartist on the loose! For Her Majesty's safety and the royal party we'd like you to follow us to the panic room.

CONROY. HE WENT THAT WAY!

LEAH *and* FRED *runs off in the direction pointed.*

DUCHESS. Albert. Victoria. You must do a duet!

VICTORIA. Er Mum –

DUCHESS (*to* GARY). Bring two grand pianos to the orangery!

GARY *exits.*

Let's give the lovers some alone time. To the chapel!

BRUNHILDA, ERNST *and* CONROY *follow the* DUCHESS *off.*

Beat.

ALBERT. What sort of music you in to?

VICTORIA. Um.

Lots of… anything I can jam to…

ALBERT. Cool. I've got loads of stuff in the locker.

Beat.

VICTORIA. That man, he was in a rage.

ALBERT. Yes, he popped all the balloons.

VICTORIA. I should have spoken to him.

ALBERT. It happened so fast.

VICTORIA. That's not an excuse.

ALBERT. Victoria… it's hard to talk to someone when they're, in pain.

VICTORIA *and* ALBERT*'s eyes catch.*

2.2

ED *walks on dressed as guard.*

He pulls VICTORIA *away from* ALBERT. *Hands her a man's shirt, jodhpurs, guard jacket, Busby, boots and a fake moustache.*

VICTORIA *dresses up.*

VICTORIA. Gotta be back in two hours.

ED. Can't promise that.

VICTORIA. My mum's poker game finishes at eleven.

ED. If I'd known she was a gambler I'd have invited her with.

VICTORIA. Er no thanks.

ED. I like mums or should I say mums like me. I once knew a mum called Francine. Used to tutor her kids. Nothing ever happened. But it was always on the cards.

VICTORIA. Don't be weird Ed.

VICTORIA *is fully dressed as a guard.*

How do I look?

ED. Like a jobsworth.

VICTORIA. Perfect.

VICTORIA *and* ED *approach the guards,* LEAH *and* FRED.

LEAH *and* FRED *have been stripped to their undergarments/underwear but they don't know this yet.*

LEAH. Where you two off to?

ED. Luigi wants us to pick up some basil.

LEAH. He's got kitchen staff for that.

ED. They're all slaving away on dinner for the card game.

LEAH. Need two of you does it?

ED. You know what it's like nowadays, wearing the uniform out and about.

VICTORIA. Protection innit.

A tense beat.

The gates open.

LEAH. Bring us back some sniff.

VICTORIA *and* ED *run out of the gates.*

FRED. Leah. Why d'you never let me do any of the talking?

FRED *looks at* LEAH, *notices she's half- naked.* LEAH *looks at* FRED, *notices he's half-naked.*

LEAH. Where are our clothes?

LEAH *and* FRED *look in the direction of where* ED *and* VICTORIA *ran.*

Look at each other. An Adam-and-Eve moment of humiliation.

Then they start taking in each other in.

Desire bubbles to the surface. They run off.

Meanwhile, VICTORIA *and* ED *adventure through London to the tune of 'The Best Things in Life are Free'.*

They arrive at a pub. There are two lonely DRINKERS. *They stare at* ED *and* VICTORIA. *Gulp.* ED *and* VICTORIA *walk to the bar. The two* DRINKERS *start to hum 'Faithful'.*

ED. Pint?

VICTORIA. Sure.

ED. Alright, Sonia.

SONIA. Do I know you?

ED. Pint of Fuller's for the lady. And for me… do you do Pinot Grigio on draught?

SONIA. You what?

ED. …Two Fuller's.

SONIA *hands them their drinks.*

The DRINKERS *continue to hum and stare at* VICTORIA.

Alright, Kev!

ED *waves at one of the lonely* DRINKERS. *The person looks right through him.*

Yeah my mum used to drink here. She would have rated you.

VICTORIA. Oh… cool.

ED. As far as boozers go it's pretty reliable. And never gets lairy on a Wednesday. How's your drink?

VICTORIA. Really lovely.

ED. Not too warm?

VICTORIA. No. I really like wine.

ED *looks at her pint of bitter.*

VICTORIA *realises she's made a mistake.* ED *smiles.*
VICTORIA *turns away mortified.*

A group of PUNTERS *arrive.*

ISABEL *and* LAURIE *bound in. They don't recognise* ED *with the beard.*

ED. Shit.

VICTORIA. What?

ED. Let's go somewhere else.

VICTORIA. We've only just arrived.

ED. I got my days mixed up! It's fight night!

VICTORIA. Sounds interesting.

ED. Trust me, you don't want to stay.

VICTORIA. Don't look now but there's a girl watching us.

In the corner, LAURIE *drinks and stares at* ED.

ED *subtly looks at* LAURIE.

Is she a friend?

ED. Not really.

VICTORIA. She's proper staring.

ED. She's drunk.

VICTORIA. Invite her over.

ED. Nobody talks to her she's a psycho.

VICTORIA (*to* LAURIE). Hello. Girl.

LAURIE *walks over.*

LAURIE (*to* ED). Who's this?

ED. This is…

VICTORIA. Clive.

LAURIE. Hello Clive. Mind fucking off for a minute?

VICTORIA. Er… sure.

VICTORIA *walks away. Sits down further off. Tries to blend in.*

ED. That was rude.

LAURIE. What's with the fake beard?

ED. Trying it for size to see if I should grow a real one.

Beat.

LAURIE. We haven't seen you in weeks. These fight nights don't run themselves.

Beat.

Are you just gonna stand there mute?

Beat.

You're my older brother, you're supposed to…

ED. Laurie, you expect too much.

LAURIE.…

ISABEL *jumps up. The pub suddenly gets very lively.*

ISABEL. Alright bets in for Dr Feel Good. Three-to-one. Three-to-one. Unbeaten in eighteen matches. Get your bets in for Dr Feel Good.

PUNTERS *gather around.*

VICTORIA. What was all that about?

ED. Just some crazy talk. Fancy a flutter?

VICTORIA. I haven't got any money.

ED. Don't worry I'll spot ya.

ED *hands* VICTORIA *some money. She runs off to bet.*

ISABEL. The Fisherman. Sixteen-to-one. Sixteen-to-one. A young fighter only his second match in the ring but very promising. Come place your bets for The Fisherman.

VICTORIA *returns to* ED.

LAURIE *sinks her pint.*

LAURIE. Tonight, we are going to witness the most anticipated match in the history of the world.

Cheers from the crowd. LAURIE *throws looks at* ED.

Ladies and gentleman, introducing first: fighting out of the corner closest to the bogs. With gold feathers and black talons. The only cock in cockfighting history to win more than eighteen consecutive matches. Please welcome to the ring DR FEEEL GOOOOOOOOOD.

A rooster, DR FEEL GOOD *clucks proudly onto the stage. His master,* NORZGARD, *attaches a silver-speared headband.*

And in the corner closest to the dartboard. With yellow feathers and blue eyelashes. The fastest kill this year, and in only his debut match. Please welcome to the ring The FIIIIISHHHERMANNNNNN.

THE FISHERMAN *clucks out onstage. His legs wobble. This is one freaked-out rooster. His mistress,* TRACEY, *attaches an identical silver-speared headband.*

Are you ready to rummmmmble?

REFEREE *jumps into the ring and address the two* COCKS.

REFEREE. I want a brave fight, no calling for Mum, your mum's dead, she ain't interested, this is your moment, all over the country cocks would give their wings for this honour, you know the rules, there are no rules, bite gouge scratch tear eat, loser joins the ancestors, winner gets a holiday.

REFEREE *blows whistle.*

The cockfight starts silly and descends into something ultra-violent.

VICTORIA. Go on Fish, you can do it, go on, good show, lovely jubbly, top work old boy, I believe in you, brilliant, you're a star, a wonder, an inspirational role model, don't even think about your opponent, he's a beardsplitter a rantallion zounderkite scobberlotcher mumblecrust go for the wobbly thing in his throat yeah fuck him up man up MAN UP PUSSY'OLE KILL KILL PENETRATE PENTRATE PENETRATE

ED *is curled up on the floor in the fetal position – not looking at the fight.*

THE FISHERMAN *kills* DR FEEL GOOD.

VICTORIA *sees* ED *sat on the floor.*

Ed.

ED *looks at* VICTORIA. *Runs off.* VICTORIA *follows him outside.*

What wrong?

ED. Nothing.

VICTORIA. Ed.

ED. Sometimes when the blood and feathers mix I have to have a lie-down.

VICTORIA. Maybe you should avoid those nights in future.

ED. Yeah.

Beat.

VICTORIA. What's the time?

ED. Late.

VICTORIA. …I should get going.

ED. I'll walk you home.

VICTORIA. No it's out of your way.

ED. Don't be silly. It's just straight down the Edgware Road.

ED *and* VICTORIA *walk home.*

(*Singing.*)
   Do I lean in and kiss her?
   Or will she call the police.
   She keeps looking around.
   Why can't I be Hercules?

   But everywhere you go,
   I could be there,
   I could be there,
   Ooo.

> Everywhere you go
> I will be there
> I will be there
> Waiting for you…

VICTORIA (*singing*).
> I wish I could rewind.
> Relive this night from the start.
> And just ask him more questions.
> Keep it straight from the heart.
>
> And everywhere you go,
> I could be there,
> I could be there,
> Ooo.

VICTORIA *and* ED (*singing*).
> Everywhere you go
> I will be there
> I will be there
> Waiting for you…

VICTORIA *and* ED *arrive at the gates.*

ED. Here we are.

VICTORIA. Yes.

Beat.

Goodnight then.

ED. Goodnight.

VICTORIA *walks in through the gates.*

2.3

In Buckingham Palace. DUCHESS, CONROY *and* GARY.

DUCHESS. I should have locked the windows. I locked the doors! But not the windows!

CONROY. She probably just went for a stroll around the gardens.

DUCHESS. That's easy for you to say micro-dick.

CONROY. Luise don't turn on me.

GARY. Would the Duchess like a slice of cake?

CONROY *holds up his hand.*

He has a moment with the DUCHESS.

CONROY. Are we any closer to my appointment?

DUCHESS. How can you be so insensitive?

CONROY. I didn't say anything. Anxiety is making you hear things.

CONROY *hugs the* DUCHESS *tight.*

VICTORIA *enters. Tries to sneak past her mother and* CONROY.

DUCHESS. VICTORIA!

DUCHESS *kisses* VICTORIA *twelve times on the forehead.*

CONROY. Why are you dressed as a jockey?

VICTORIA. I've been horse-riding.

CONROY. We checked the barn.

VICTORIA. I was in the stables. With a horse.

CONROY. Doing what?

VICTORIA. Singing to it.

CONROY *and* DUCHESS *look at each other.*

Mum, can I go to bed?

DUCHESS. Gary.

GARY. Duchess.

DUCHESS. Make sure she brushes her teeth has her vitamins uses the toilet it's a warm night so let's go for the flowery silk PJs. And a German lullaby. She's getting rusty.

GARY *bows*.

GARY *and* VICTORIA *exit*.

Beat.

CONROY. There's been sightings of a boy around the Palace. Lady Sandwich saw him on top of a chimney looking at the moon. A chambermaid heard someone chewing very loudly underneath a chaise longue. I'm going to recruit a special unit of soldiers.

DUCHESS. Soldiers? That's a bit paranoid.

CONROY. The Palace has turned into a summer camp. Tonight I found two guards copulating.

DUCHESS. Which ones?

CONROY. Leah and Fred.

DUCHESS. I hope you disciplined them.

CONROY. Oh yes.

DUCHESS. Deploying soldiers isn't exactly subtle.

CONROY. They won't look like soldiers. It will be very off-book.

DUCHESS. Isn't this how revolutions start?

CONROY. I'm more interested in your safety.

There's a boy running around this Palace whenever he chooses. The *Herald* call him a Chartist. The *Mercury* calls him Peter Pan. None of this bodes well for your little girl.

DUCHESS. Soldiers in the Palace, it doesn't feel right.

CONROY. My love we need to catch him A-S-A-P. Nip this story in the bud before the rest of England gets ideas.

Pause.

DUCHESS. Take off your shirt.

CONROY *unbuttons his shirt.*

Get the marmalade and the shoe.

CONROY. Meet you in the Billiards room in five.

CONROY *and* DUCHESS *exit.*

Darkness in the Palace. Everyone is asleep.

Only GARY *is awake… singing a German lullaby.*

It is pure and delicate.

More ominous sounds creep in.

CECIL *and* SASHA *walk on.* CECIL *has a yoyo.*

3.1

VICTORIA *wears a bathrobe. She has just got out of the shower. Her hair is wet. She walks slowly and upright, practising a walk.*

Outside the bathroom, GARY *sits with a towel.*

ED *shoots out of the chimney into* VICTORIA*'s bathroom. He is covered in soot and grease.* VICTORIA *doesn't notice, she is concentrating on her walk.* ED *watches her.*

VICTORIA *turns around, sees* ED, *screams, immediately puts her hand over her mouth.*

GARY. Your Majesty did you fall over?

VICTORIA. No.

GARY. Your Majesty, should I come in?

VICTORIA. No!

GARY. I heard a scream –

VICTORIA. No scream.

GARY. It sounded a bit like 'aaaah'.

VICTORIA. Yeah that… that was just um… *me* time.

   Beat.

ED. Didn't know the chimney would take me into your bathroom.

VICTORIA. Oh really?

ED. Good bath?

VICTORIA. Wait how long have you been watching?

ED. No – I literally – just arrived.

   Beat.

Big day tomorrow.

VICTORIA. Yep.

ED. Suppose you've been prepping your entire life.

VICTORIA. Since I was twelve.

ED. Are you up for it though?

VICTORIA. What?

ED. Being Queen, are you up for it?

VICTORIA. Yeah obviously.

I tried the corset on this morning. It's a joke. It's basically asking my body to squeeze something out.

ED. If anyone can get away with farting in the Abbey you can.

GARY. Your Majesty you ready for drying?

VICTORIA. IN A MINUTE!

ED. You ever thought about getting your own bedroom?

VICTORIA. Why would I need my own bedroom?

ED. Oh I dunno.

Pause.

We could go to Blackpool.

VICTORIA. Blackpool the holiday destination?

ED. Yeah, go for a weekend.

VICTORIA. For a holiday?

ED. Or the rest of our lives.

'The Best Things in Life are Free' starts to underscore.

See you tomorrow then.

VICTORIA. There's four hundred thousand people coming, I might not.

ED. I'll do something fucking mad so you do.

GARY. Your Majesty you'll turn into a prune!

VICTORIA. I'M SHAVING! Is there anyone in your lineage who might be like a lord?

ED. My mum and dad met in an asylum.

VICTORIA. Wow. Grandparents?

ED. I come from a long list of nobodies.

VICTORIA. Shame.

ED. That could change for my offspring.

VICTORIA. How?

ED (*rapping*).
> You gotta grab it, take it, touch it, taste it,
> Put it in your mouth and try not to break it,
> Feel the breeze between your thighs, stretch those legs and make you exercise,
> I'm gonna bend you, flip you, pull you, toss you
> Trust me Vicky I promise not to drop you
> Stick to me, like birds to bees, eventually we'll have kids-to-be.

(*Singing.*)
> The best things in life are free my Queen, if you want to find out all you gotta do is follow me.

VICTORIA (*rapping*).
> Boy break in my bathroom, think he a big man
> Running his mouth like he's dancing the can-can
> Girl got standards, I'm looking for heartfelt.
> A spiritual ting not just a notch on your belt.
> So there's the chimney, it's time you climb.
> And who knows one day you may be mine.

ED (*rapping*).
> So tonight you're sending me back to my slum.

VICTORIA (*rapping*).
> I'd only shag you tonight to piss off my mum.

ED *and* VICTORIA (*singing*).

> The best things in life are free my Queen, if you wanna
> > find out all you gotta do is follow me.
> The best things in life are free my Queen –

GARY. YOUR MAJESTY I'M ABOUT TO BREAK DOWN THE DOOR.

VICTORIA *walks very close to* ED.

VICTORIA. See ya.

VICTORIA *walks off.*

ED *does a little dance. A mixture of joy and sexual frustration.*

SASHA *and* CECIL *enter. See* ED.

ED *leaves, unaware he is being followed.*

3.2

In an antechamber in Westminster Abbey, VICTORIA *is being dressed for her coronation by her ladies-in-waiting.*

Outside in the street are the CHARTISTS.

CHARTISTS (*singing.*)

> There's a fire burning deep within the city,
> Full of rage at endless days of misery.
> New Queen Vic, you could shake things up,
> Give us the vote girl, show us what you've got.
>
> Kids are starving, while you're sipping on ye tea,
> Summer picnics, Corgis on your knee,
> We've been bruised, blood red and blue
> Give us the vote girl, or we'll come for you.
>
> Don't be scared Vic, we don't wanna bite,
> Come out and talk to us, there's no need to fight.

But stay in hiding, we'll be here all night.
Yes stay in hiding, we'll be here all night.

VICTORIA *tries to run away. Her* LADIES *wrestle her to the ground.* VICTORIA *is forced to walk up the aisle.*

VICTORIA *enters to an awe-inspiring choral number. She is kissed by hundreds.*

LAURIE *and* ISABEL *have managed to get into the Abbey. They stand at the back, very still. They look like they've not slept in days. They stare at* VICTORIA.

Two drunk REVELLERS *drag off the* ARCHBISHOP OF CANTERBURY.

A moment later, a REVELLER *appears, dressed as the Archbishop. He cracks open a beer. The fizz echoes around the silent Abbey. A thousand eyes fall on him.*

REVELLER. I now pronounce you, Queen Victoria. Queen of England, Scotland, Ireland and Wales.

3.3

A dungeon in the basement of the Palace.

ED *is tied up. In the shadows stand* CECIL *and* SASHA.

CONROY *enters straight from the coronation. Inspects* ED.

SASHA. Edward Jones. From Kilburn. Unemployed.

CONROY. That didn't take long.

SASHA. He was very obliging.

CONROY. Well Edward Jones, your little jolly is over. That's your fifteen minutes of fame done. Sasha hand him directly to the police.

SASHA. Lord Conroy may I make a suggestion?

CONROY. Go on.

SASHA. Let's keep him here overnight.

CONROY. Is that necessary?

SASHA. A lot of young people are handed over to the police and given a caution which amounts to nothing more than a smacked bottom. They are then released back into society and carry on doing whatever they've been doing. This isn't the occasion for a proper debate around crime and punishment, but allow Cecil and I some time with him, and he'll never break into the Palace again.

CONROY. Is that a code for murder?

SASHA. God no, we're not murderers.

CONROY. Well what are you going to do?

SASHA. It'll be a surprise.

CONROY. Mummy once threw me a surprise party and when everybody screamed 'Surprise!', Daddy dropped dead.

SASHA. Our condolences.

CONROY. Thank you. *So tell me*.

Beat.

SASHA. Might be easier to show you.

SASHA ties ED's hands behind his back.

SASHA takes out a lunchbox with a bottle of milk and a pot of honey.

Paints ED's face with milk and honey.

CONROY. I'd like to lick him, but is that what you're going for?

SASHA. In three days this boy will have no face. Flies, maggots, rats will eat it.

Beat.

CONROY. Remarkable. What do you do Cecil during all of this?

CECIL. I just play with my yoyo.

SASHA. Witnessing such innocence whilst being eaten alive is unbearable.

CONROY. If anyone ever hears about this, we'll be hanged.

Keep him here a day then hand him over.

SASHA. Could we have a day and a half?

CONROY *waves an approval and walks off.*

3.4

VICTORIA *post-coronation, in her bedroom alone.*

She puts her hand in an ice bucket.

DUCHESS *enters.*

DUCHESS. Where's my bed?

VICTORIA. Yeah. Um. It's been moved.

DUCHESS. Moved?

VICTORIA. To storage.

DUCHESS. What?

VICTORIA. I've given you your own room. With a new bed. The Nash Suite… it's lighter and –

DUCHESS. You've moved me into another room!?

VICTORIA. It's only down the corridor.

DUCHESS. Why?

VICTORIA. I thought it'd be nice for you to have your own space Mum. Isn't it, isn't it, isn't it time you moved on from the camp bed?

DUCHESS. But I like my camp bed.

VICTORIA. Well I'll get Gary to retrieve it from storage and install it in the Nash.

DUCHESS. Gary!?

GARY *enters*.

DUCHESS. Go bring my camp bed back in here.

VICTORIA. Gary, no. The Duchess will be staying in the Nash Suite.

That's all.

GARY. Your Majesty.

GARY *bows and exits*.

DUCHESS (*in German*). What's going on Victoria?

VICTORIA. I'm eighteen.

DUCHESS (*in German*). So!?

VICTORIA. ...it's time I slept on my own.

DUCHESS (*in German*). Who put these sick thoughts into your head!?

VICTORIA. Nobody put these thoughts in my head!?

DUCHESS (*in German*). You think you'll sleep without me!?

VICTORIA. I'd like to try.

DUCHESS (*in German*). You're too fragile.

VICTORIA. Why can't I try?

DUCHESS. Years ago you tried to sleep on your own and you nearly set yourself on fire.

VICTORIA. I kicked over a candle!

DUCHESS (*in German*). Let me feel your head.

DUCHESS *feels* VICTORIA*'s head*.

Oh my love. You're hot.

VICTORIA. Don't you dare.

DUCHESS. Burning up.

VICTORIA. (*Liar!*)

> VICTORIA *takes her hand out of the ice bucket and pulls off the ruby ring.*

DUCHESS. You've always had fat fingers. It's why you didn't take to the piano.

VICTORIA. The Archbishop put the ring on the wrong finger!

> *Beat.*

> (*In German.*) Don't you want to sleep on your own?

DUCHESS (*in German*). You're my girl, why would I want to sleep on my own?

VICTORIA. Mum I need to –

DUCHESS. Wait is this about getting a man?

VICTORIA. You're missing the point.

DUCHESS. It's only a matter of time before you and Albert are an *item*.

VICTORIA. I'm not marrying Albert.

DUCHESS. Do you want a woman?

VICTORIA. No I just… need to do my own thing.

DUCHESS (*in German*). What does that mean?

VICTORIA. I need to be on my own.

> *Beat.*

> DUCHESS *faints.*

> Get up.

DUCHESS. I've fainted.

VICTORIA. GET UP.

> DUCHESS *gets up.*

DUCHESS. A parent gives a child roots and wings.

VICTORIA. So give me wings!?

DUCHESS. Yours were damaged when you came out of me. I knew something was wrong, on my breast you went blue, I thought that was it, but then from somewhere deep, a roar. (*In German*.) And then I wiped your bum, breastfed, played, educated, left my home sacrificed everything and yet now now now now now when my little girl becomes Queen she thinks – (*In English*.) she thinks that she can just kick me out into the street like a dog!?

VICTORIA. Your new bed is really bouncy.

DUCHESS. Don't make jokes. Don't be English. Don't be small and English and make fucking jokes.

VICTORIA. Mum you didn't want a daughter, you wanted a doll.

DUCHESS....

VICTORIA....

DUCHESS (*singing*).
    My bird is flying the nest,
    Now what do I have left?
    My little girl
    You were sweet like a cinnamon swirl.
    You were sweet like a cinnamon swirl.

    But you grow, yeah you grow
    Into a girl I barely know
    And you grow, yeah you grow,
    Oh you grow.

    Okay I'll move to the Nash,
    But please let me come back and crash,
    In the morning, brunch and chats
    In the evening, a milky snack
    Those midnight hours we'll never get back.

    But you grow, yeah you grow
    Into a girl I barely know
    And you grow, yeah could grow,
    Oh you grow.

VICTORIA. I know where this is going.

DUCHESS (*singing*).
>I won't go quietly into the night
>Girls from Coburg know how to fight.
>Don't be fooled by my sweet veneer,
>I'll spare no mercy if you wound my heart,
>wound my heart, wound my heart

VICTORIA. Gary!

DUCHESS (*singing*).
>I've given you my trust
>Maybe too much
>Is this how you repay?
>All of my love.
>I will not rest
>Mother knows best
>Mother knows best
>Mother knows best

GARY arrives.

GARY. Your Majesty.

VICTORIA. Escort the Duchess to the Nash Suite.

Music stops.

DUCHESS (*singing*).
>You fucking what, you little snake.
>You little bitch, I hate your face.
>With your tiny mind and your massive pig's trotters,
>Thank god your dad's dead, for he'd die again, die again,
>   die again.

VICTORIA. Gary remove her!

The DUCHESS *growls at* GARY.

GARY *carries the* DUCHESS *off.*

VICTORIA *is alone. She shouts up the chimney.*

Yo Ed. Mission accomplished.

Ed?

(*Singing*.)
> The room seems dark and cold,
> Now I've been brave and bold,
> It's time to put this silly crush on hold.
> I'll meet with my Prime Minister
> Talk matters of the state.
> Engage the Chartists in honest debate.

(*Spoken*.) But.

(*Singing*.)
> Where is he? My symphony.

3.5

A prison cell.

LEN *is engaged in an activity.*

ED *is thrown in the cell. Half of his face is missing.* (*It's been eaten.*)

LEN. Rough night?

ED....

LEN. I'm Len.

Beat.

What are you in for?

ED. Stop talking to me.

LEN. There's no one else to talk to.

ED. Don't you have exercises to do?

LEN. These opportunities don't come around every day.

ED. Are you a paedo?

LEN. No.

ED. So what's with all the chat?

LEN. I've been in solitary for quite a while.

ED. – ?

LEN. I'm a danger to other prisoners. I have ideas that if shared could result in officers being burnt.

ED. They put *me* in here. You can't be that dangerous.

LEN. There's two possible reasons for that. Either the prison has run out of cells, or you're such a cretin they don't think you'll understand the People's Charter.

ED. Jesus hear enough of your rubbish at home.

LEN. Chartist family!?

ED. Look Mr –

LEN. Call me Len.

ED. I'm not interested in your ideas.

LEN. Why they're brilliant.

ED. Romanticise the working man go on I'll get a semi.

LEN. We've got all night for that.

ED. I've got a knife in my sock.

LEN. Me too. Who did that to your face?

ED. ....

LEN. Cos that's where your anger should be directed.

Pause.

ED. When's supper?

LEN. In about fourteen hours.

ED. That would make it breakfast.

LEN. (Yes.)

In the afternoon I'm allowed out in the yard for half an hour. I have to keep my distance. Five feet. I can't really proselytise in those conditions but I do hear the odd bit of gossip. There's a rumour about a boy caught wandering around Buckingham Palace.

ED. What were they saying about him?

LEN. That he was tortured by Palace security.

ED. ....

LEN. The tabloids are licking their lips. Palace security doing the job of the police. Could be the start of a civil war. I can't thank you enough.

Beat.

ED. How long you in here for?

LEN. Still waiting for a trial.

ED. What did you do?

LEN. I had the balls to look the Queen in the eye.

Beat.

Ever seen her in the flesh?

ED. No.

LEN. One day hey?

ED. ....

LEN. Better get in there quick before the cousin does.

ED. Keep talking and I'll cut you.

Beat.

'Faithful' underscores.

LEN. Boyo Jones is what they're calling you. You have a nickname. Now I'm both attracted and repulsed by celebrity gossip, but let us say there's a sliver of truth. And let us say you're able to break into the Palace. And let us also say you have access to the Queen. On release shouldn't you go and talk to her. Tell her about how you've suffered. Why settle for this pain? In the blink of an eye she can change your world. And she can change ours.

Beat.

Three OFFICERS *enter the cell. Two carry large cannonballs. Drop them by the feet of* ED *and* LEN.

OFFICER TROY *stays. The other two leave.*

ED *and* LEN *pick up and drop the cannonballs. They do this action on repeat.*

OFFICER TROY *sits and watches.*

Blackout.

4.1

LEAH *is showing* VICTORIA *around a flat in Blackpool.*
VICTORIA *is in disguise.*

LEAH. So this is one of our larger studios. I'd actually say it
feels more like a one-bed. Great views of the sea. You never
get bored of looking at the sea. Did you say you were from
London?

VICTORIA *smiles and nods.*

I used to live in London.

The landlord actually refurbished last year. Lovely finishes.
A lot of flats in the area – first time to Blackpool?

VICTORIA *nods.*

A lot of flats in Blackpool are real hell-holes. The landlords
don't even bother charging deposits so you can imagine the
type of tenant they're willing to accept – seen many other
flats?

VICTORIA *shakes her head.*

Well take my word for it I wouldn't bother. I've seen flats
with human faeces, condoms, dead animals. Bathroom tiles
stained with blood. People come to Blackpool to die. But
loads also come for their holidays. Will you be living alone
or with somebody?

VICTORIA. With my boyfriend.

LEAH. The size makes it ideal for a couple. I'm happy to
arrange a second viewing if he's around?

VICTORIA. He's not. At the moment.

LEAH. Does he live in London too?

VICTORIA *nods*.

I had a fella when I lived in London. Fred. He had these blond curls that I had stop myself from continually twirling.

LEAH *looks at* VICTORIA. *A moment.*

You're my sixth viewing today – it's a very popular block – so if you're at all interested I'd recommend acting fast.

VICTORIA. How many rooms in the flat?

LEAH. Well just this one because it is technically a studio.

VICTORIA. Could I see the parlour?

LEAH. There isn't a… parlour. There's a shared garden

VICTORIA. Shared with whom?

LEAH. …the other tenants in the block.

VICTORIA. When you say other tenants do you mean staff?

Pause.

LEAH. Your Majesty what are you doing in Blackpool?

VICTORIA. Um. Call me Victoria. I'm. I'm. Sorry what's your name?

LEAH. Don't be sorry I only worked for you for eight years. Leah.

VICTORIA. Leah. Between you and me… I'm considering moving here.

LEAH. Right.

VICTORIA. I think it might be easier to make a go of it with the boyfriend.

LEAH. Well it is a very romantic town, and you're a five-minute walk from the pleasure beach – sorry this is totally fucking insane. Why not live with your fella in Buckingham Palace!?

VICTORIA. I can't.

LEAH. But you're the Queen!?

A moment where VICTORIA *hears* ED *singing.*

VICTORIA. Not for much longer.

Pause.

LEAH. Do you want to have a moment alone in the flat? I always advise prospective tenants to just spend some time imagining their lives here.

VICTORIA *nods.*

And I can waive the tenancy agreement. No problem.

LEAH *walks off.*

VICTORIA *spends some time imagining herself in the flat.*

4.2

A visiting room in the prison.

TONI *is an expensively dressed American. She is sat opposite* ED.

OFFICER TROY *stands at a distance, monitoring.*

ED (*to* OFFICER TROY). Can I go back to my cell?

OFFICER TROY. Miss Toni has paid for the hour.

TONI *apprises* ED *in silence.*

TONI. You are a specimen and when my people *see you* and *hear you* they will forget their worries and travel to somewhere sublime without ever leaving their seats.

ED. Are you mentally unwell?

TONI. I think we're all mentally unwell. We are mental creatures. Life throws curveballs and they hit us squarely in the face. Some of us haemorrhage on the spot. Others just need to lie down. Take a time-out. Meditate. I think you belong in the latter camp. You're a spiritual person, I can see it in your eyes. They're burning into my soul.

ED. Officer Troy please.

OFFICER TROY. Do you want to keep your testicles?

TONI. Officer Troy! You get straight to the heart of things.

OFFICER TROY. Thank you madam.

TONI. Ed. Eddie. Eduardo. What happened in the Palace?

ED. I already told you.

TONI. Any more details?

ED. No.

TONI. Dreams nightmares fantasies I'll take anything.

ED. Nothing happened in the Palace!

Beat.

TONI. What I'm about to say might sound implausible. I own a theatre in New York. It's well known around the world for its variety acts, musicals, freak shows. I'd like to create a show inspired by your life.

ED. This is bollocks.

TONI. Hold on there amigo. I'd also like you to come to New York and appear in the show every night.

ED. Like acting?

TONI. You'd be playing yourself.

ED. Huh?

TONI. The central story will be a relationship between a hobo and the Queen –

ED. I'm not a hobo.

TONI. Course not, you live in Kilburn, am I saying that correctly?

OFFICER TROY. Yes.

TONI. But it'll make a better show if you are a hobo.

ED. Please let me go back to my cell.

TONI. Hear me out cowboy! The Queen and the hobo will be played by professional circus artists. The audience will be spellbound by this fairytale romance and you won't be required till the curtain call, when you'll appear in a luminous box and everything will become hyper-real.

ED. I don't like boxes, I don't like crowds, I don't like the sea.

TONI. None of that is set in stone.

ED. I don't like Americans.

TONI. I'd be willing to pay two pounds per week.

Beat.

ED. What do I have to do?

TONI. Descend in a luminous palace from the rafters. Are you scared of heights?

ED. No.

TONI. Wonderful.

ED. Two pounds a week for just standing in a box?

TONI. Waving to the crowds, possibly singing 'I'm Boy Jones, we made love on the throne.'

ED. But I didn't!

TONI. It's a story!

ED. Is this some sick joke?

TONI. Oh no I'm deadly serious. I almost never do jokes. And when I do. You'll know I'm doing one.

ED. Look where I am…

TONI. I've spoken to a lawyer. It's only a matter of time till you're released.

ED. It's been three months and no trial.

TONI. They have nothing on you. Anyways. I'd like to open the show next fall.

Beat.

ED. A show about my life?

TONI. Yes sir.

ED. Then why mention Victoria?

TONI. Americans are going batshit for your Queen.

ED. She's a demon.

TONI. Well the show would mostly be about you.

ED. Why not make it *all* about me?

TONI. It will be all about you.

ED. Whose face will be on the poster!?

TONI. Both!

ED. Why her face!? Everybody already knows her face! Nobody knows mine! I, I'm wasting away in here, I'm being forgotten.

TONI. I'm going to make the world remember you.

ED. It's too late, she, she (forgot).

Beat.

Leave me alone.

TONI. Let me help you.

ED. You can't.

Beat.

TONI (*to* OFFICER TROY). What's bail posted at?

OFFICER TROY. I'll have to enquire Miss Toni.

TONI (*to* ED). This is the sort of opportunity you need to talk about with family.

4.3

ED *has a rucksack on.* ISABEL *and* LAURIE *are looking at him.*

ISABEL. All packed?

ED *nods.*

I'll walk you to the train.

ED *shakes his head.*

LAURIE. Ed. It's gonna be incredible.

Beat.

ED. You're against the Queen, but when an American flashes her cash your tongues are out like dogs.

LAURIE. They're entirely separate predicaments.

ED. I think you pick and choose.

LAURIE. Everyone picks and chooses.

ISABEL. You should get going. Miss your train and you'll miss the boat.

ED. When the American talked about me coming down in a box, I started seeing a cage. You hear horror stories over there about people in cages.

LAURIE. You'll be alright you're British.

ED. I can't go.

LAURIE. What?

ED. I can't leave.

ISABEL. Are you scared of the sea?

ED. I've got things to do, here.

LAURIE. What have you got to do!?

Beat.

ED. At least let me have a last smoke.

LAURIE *takes out an opium pipe. Lights it up.*

The three siblings pass it around, smoking.

SASHA *and* CECIL *arrive outside the siblings' home. They have binoculars. Perhaps the type you find at the opera. A stake-out begins.*

ISABEL. This is strong stuff.

LAURIE. Yeah watch it... new batch... makes you see things.

Long pause.

ED. Don't make me go.

LAURIE. There's nothing for you here.

ISABEL. Apart from people laughing at you.

LAURIE. Do the job for a year and you'll never have to work again.

ED. And *you'll* never have to work again. I'm not going.

Pause.

ISABEL. At the end with Mum.

With those one-on-ones.

She told me to look out for you.

ED....

ISABEL. Said you'd end up in a ditch if we weren't careful.

LAURIE. Isabel those conversations were private.

ISABEL. That you were always in your head... a dreamer... and from afar it's charming but what it actually means is, you really don't care about anyone.

ED. Mum said that?

ISABEL. I feel bad telling you.

ED. Nice try Isabel. Using our dead mum.

ISABEL. How the fuck are we related?

ED. I dunno. I eat novels for breakfast you can barely spell your name.

LAURIE. Everyone calm down! Ed this is a gig you throw your lover under a train for. A show in New York! Thousands of people will come and watch you *be paid to act*! But forget the money for a sec, after the show you'll be greeted by fans, not crazies who harass you but actual fans who adore you, and producers will take you to dinners and buy you drinks and offer you edgy-yet-mainstream projects and after you'll meet up with friends and go to parties, see someone across the room, go over to them and laugh about nothing and talk very seriously about the world and have proper sex that lasts until morning no rushing to work at 6 a.m. sleep in late wake up next to that someone, and it isn't awkward, or it is fucking awkward but you still go out for brunch and read the papers and drink orange juice in the *autumnal sun*!

LAURIE *looks at her opium pipe. Whoa.*

ISABEL *checks her watch.*

ISABEL. We're late.

LAURIE. Shit.

ISABEL *and* LAURIE *take out compacts and begin to apply make-up.*

ED *watches.*

(*To* ED.) If only we had a shilling, all our debts to the wicked men would be paid.

4.4

ED *and* VICTORIA *alone for the first time in her bedroom.*

VICTORIA. You took your time.

ED. I've been in prison.

VICTORIA....

ED. Didn't you know?

VICTORIA. I thought it was just the tabloids chatting shit.

ED. Really.

VICTORIA. Ed, if I'd've known I would've definitely... your face. You going for a 'Hunchback of Notre Dame' look?

ED....

VICTORIA. Bit soon? (For a joke.)

ED *nods.*

How did you get in?

ED. Nightmare journey. All the chimneys've been lit. I had to cover myself in bear grease and shimmy through some window bars in the scullery. A chef saw me – thought I worked here – standard – got me making cranberry tarts which by the way oooof. Anyway. Enough about the commute.

Here I am.

VICTORIA. Here you are.

ED. In your own bedroom.

VICTORIA. Finally.

Pause.

ED. Do you like sleeping on your own?

VICTORIA. Getting used to it. It was hard at first.

ED. How come?

VICTORIA. I was er breastfed till I was eight so got some issues.

Pause.

ED. Most mornings I read the papers. Gives me tingles to read about my exploits.

VICTORIA. So you're a narcissist.

ED. I suppose. But it's more of a laugh. The shit they make up. They really have no idea about us.

VICTORIA. '*Us*'?

ED. That we know each other. That we…

It's like beyond their imagination.

VICTORIA. Needs to stay that way.

ED. Does it?

VICTORIA. Yes.

ED. They say I'm an asexual urchin who only breaks in for cheese.

VICTORIA. Who cares what they write?

ED. Read about your cousin Albert coming to visit *again*. What's that all about?

Beat.

They're saying it's just a formality before a proposal.

VICTORIA. Are you jealous?

ED. Do you like him?

VICTORIA. … not in that way.

ED. We could come clean about what we are and put all those rumours –

VICTORIA. What we are, I mean we aren't, wait, what?

ED *gets down on one knee.*

ED. Queen Victoria would you do me the honour of –

VICTORIA. Whoa.

ED. Ah!?

VICTORIA. Get up.

ED. Sorry –

VICTORIA. No Ed it's –

ED. Totally misread –

VICTORIA. No I like, shit –

ED. FUUUUUUUUCK!

Beat.

VICTORIA. It's cool. Just, it's yeah, there's stuff that's beyond my (control) I mean I need to get my head – I need to get a grip on what is going in my own Palace and like you swan in here all loose and who who who do you think you are?

Beat.

ED. An American producer wants me to star in a show in New York! She was gonna pay me two pounds a week but then she started throwing around stupid numbers. I could probably buy Buckingham Palace in a year.

VICTORIA. Congratulations.

ED. I turned her down.

VICTORIA. That was dumb.

ED. I told her I preferred to spend my days getting my face eaten.

VICTORIA. I didn't know anything about that!

ED. It happened in your fucking basement!

VICTORIA. I've pardoned your sentence by the way –

ED. I thought you didn't know –

VICTORIA. I didn't, but then I was told you were given bail and a trial date and I've since been able to pardon your crime, not that it's a crime, there's no need to thank me.

ED. I was in there for three months!

Beat.

VICTORIA. You should take up the American's offer of New York.

ED. Too late now.

Pause.

VICTORIA. I've got a knot in my hair. Would you comb it out?

ED. Er… yeah.

ED *combs* VICTORIA*'s hair for a very long time.*

Turns her around. Smiles.

On his exit, ED *takes a jizzy condom from his pocket and drops it on the floor.*

4.5

CONROY *enters with parchment. Sees the jizzy condom on the floor. Picks it up with a quill.*

CONROY. I wonder who's that is?

VICTORIA. Are you still sleeping with my mum?

CONROY. Now and then.

CONROY *takes out an evidence bag and pockets the condom.*

Beat.

VICTORIA. I won't be making you private secretary.

CONROY *picks up a pillow.*

CONROY. Oooh Vic, remember the fun we'd have with this – (*Indicating pillow.*)

You used to dress up as a nun and chase me around the room. Why a nun, who knows?

VICTORIA. I was a kid.

CONROY. Good times. I've not hit you with one of these for ages. May I?

VICTORIA. I'd rather you didn't.

CONROY. Okay Queeny.

Now. A little security update. The Boy Jones is out and about. There was a sighting this morning.

VICTORIA. He's harmless.

CONROY. Know him do you?

VICTORIA. No!

CONROY. Met him have you?

VICTORIA. Never.

CONROY. Then how do you know he's harmless.

VICTORIA. All he seems to do is borrow books or eat mutton.

CONROY. He shat on the throne.

VICTORIA. What?

CONROY. Earlier today someone shat on the throne. I can't think of any other culprits apart from Boy Jones.

VICTORIA. It might have been Dash.

CONROY. I know what dogshit looks like.

VICTORIA. We need to focus on other matters.

CONROY. He poses a threat to national security.

VICTORIA. How!?

CONROY. I need your signature here.

VICTORIA. What am I signing?

CONROY. An order to shoot terrorists on sight.

VICTORIA. NO!

Beat.

CONROY. When you discovered you were next in line you cried on my shoulder.

VICTORIA….?

CONROY. Were they tears of joy? Or fear?

VICTORIA….?

CONROY. It's a joyful and fearful thing to assume the crown. But there's no getting around it. People want to hurt you. This Boy Jones, he's unstoppable he seems to be able to walk through walls. What else has he walked through?

Beat.

VICTORIA. I'm not going to murder civilians.

CONROY. The soldiers I've recruited will die for you.

VICTORIA. It's gone wrong somewhere. The Palace should feel more open.

CONROY. Then you'll be dead in a month.

VICTORIA. What!? Why?

CONROY. An open Palace means people get to know you. They'll see that you eat sleep and shit the same. Then they'll think: 'Why should she live in a house with seven hundred and seventy-five rooms?' It's why you have to marry an equal. The moment ordinary people recognise you as *them*, they'll murder you.

Beat.

Sign. Stay safe.

Beat.

VICTORIA *reads the document.*

Rips it up into little pieces.

CONROY *begins to beat* VICTORIA *with the pillow. Feathers fly out.*

VICTORIA *manages to get hold of the pillow. She hits* CONROY *back. Again and again and again.*

VICTORIA. Touch Boy Jones again and I'll have you arrested.

Exits.

CECIL (*singing*).
     The long road to progress is paved with little fools,
     Don't let this little girl control you.
     You're building a better world,
     A world that's free from fear,
     It's time for Boy Jones to disappear.

CONROY. We can't – it would be the end of us.

CECIL. There are many ways for someone to disappear.

CECIL, SASHA *and* CONROY (*singing*).
     We'll stand tall, won't let her fall.
     We'll stand tall, and build a wall.

5.1

ALBERT *and* VICTORIA.

VICTORIA. When we first met I thought you were a tool.

ALBERT. Don't hold back.

VICTORIA. Maybe I was a little hasty.

So, Albert.

ALBERT. ...that's my name.

VICTORIA. Does anyone ever call you Bert?

ALBERT. No.

Pause.

VICTORIA. How many children do you want?

ALBERT. Um... I've never given it much thought.

VICTORIA. Give it some now.

Beat.

ALBERT. I'd like a big family.

A bit more than a string quartet, bit less than a brass band.

VICTORIA. Can you be more specific?

ALBERT. ...Six children. Three boys. Three girls. But Victoria surely this would be up for discussion.

How many children would you like?

VICTORIA. I dunno.

Maybe nine.

But then again I'm really not broody. Sometimes I walk through Hyde Park and see these mums with their babies, all cocooned in their own private worlds. It's something out of a horror show.

Beat.

What's your favourite food?

ALBERT. Mutton. Do you like...?

VICTORIA. Yes. Very much.

ALBERT. When I was younger we'd have it every Sunday.

VICTORIA. How lovely.

ALBERT. I suppose you ate it whenever you wanted.

VICTORIA. (No.) For ages I was on a strict diet of bread and milk.

Beat.

What does God lack?

ALBERT. This is feeling like a test.

VICTORIA. It is. What does God lack?

ALBERT. ....limitations.

VICTORIA. Pretty good.

ALBERT. We could get to know each other more naturally rather than running through a checklist of questions.

VICTORIA. Yeah that doesn't really work for me.

ALBERT. Why not?

VICTORIA. Because ultimately I need to know very quickly whether we share the same worldview. Let's not beat around the bush. You come from a horrible marriage. Did your parents even have the conversation we're having?

Beat.

ALBERT. You're very cold.

VICTORIA. Am I?

Beat.

ALBERT. Love, romance, whatever you want to call it might not sustain a marriage, but you do need it to kick things off.

VICTORIA. Okay.

ALBERT. Okay?

VICTORIA. You see romance in operas.

ALBERT. That's a version of romance.

VICTORIA. I hear you're in to shells.

ALBERT. Yes I collect.

VICTORIA. If I was to clear Brighton Beach of shells and then display them in a newly built gallery, for your eyes only, would that be romantic?

ALBERT. Sort of.

VICTORIA. Cool.

ALBERT. Please don't do that.

VICTORIA. Course not. The people of Brighton would have my head on a spike.

Beat.

ALBERT. Now it's my turn. May I borrow your musicians?

VICTORIA. Sure.

The string quartet enter.

ALBERT (*singing*).
        I'd like to tell the story
        Of us in years to come
        How we built a life
        How it all began

        Let's have a simple wedding,
        Or we could invite the nation.
        Before retiring to our beds,
        For quiet *contemplation*.

All I want to know, is will you spend your life with me?
I want to be by your side, in this cloudy country
All I want to say, is I'll always be here for you
Standing by your side – I know we can see this through
Ohhhh, ohhhh.

I can promise you
That I will never lie
What I'm feeling right now
It will last until I die.

Why not grow old together?
Take our place amongst the stars
Looking down on a dynasty
That we can call ours

All I want to know, is will you spend your life with me?
I want to be by your side, in this fine country.
All I want to say, is I'll always be here for you
Standing by your side – I know that we can see this
    through.

VICTORIA *makes a decision.*

5.2

A dungeon at the bottom of the Palace.

ISABEL *and* LAURIE *are on chairs with their hands tied
behind their backs, and hessian sacks cover their faces.*

CECIL *plays with her yoyo.*

Silence.

SASHA *pushes a garden shed onstage.*

SASHA (*to* ISABEL *and* LAURIE). Grandma was an avid
    gardener. Of a Saturday, she'd potter around the allotment
    for hours. Talking to herself, talking to the vegetables,

talking to the little boy kept in the shed. I don't have
Grandma's passion for horticulture but I do enjoy using her
tools in *my work*.

In memory of Grandma, permit me to introduce the tools
with their Latin names.

(*In Latin*.) Gardening gloves, a trowel, thermos, secateurs,
shears, shovel, rake, hoe.

(*In English*.) Chainsaw. Forgive me I don't know the Latin
phrase. It's a German invention. Very new to market. Let's
see now. The Latin for chain is torque –

CONROY'S VOICE. Stop yapping Sasha.

SASHA. Apologies Lord Conroy.

CONROY'S VOICE. Bring out Boy Jones.

ISABEL *and* LAURIE *react underneath their hessian sacks.*

SASHA *brings* ED *out of the garden shed.*

Stop.

ED *stops.*

Sit.

ED *sits.*

Looks at the sacks and realises they're his siblings.

ED *vomits.*

I'm going to you ask some questions. Tell the truth your
siblings will be released unharmed. If you lie, they won't.

Beat.

Are you a Chartist?

ED. No.

CONROY'S VOICE. You're lying.

ED. I have sympathies, nothing more.

CONROY'S VOICE. What are you then?

ED. I'm a tailor architect lover philosopher poet journalist rent-boy priest.

CONROY'S VOICE. Sasha, a finger.

SASHA *does something horrible to one of* ISABEL*'s fingers.*

What do you think of the Queen?

ED. She-she-she's the Queen.

CONROY'S VOICE. What does that mean?

ED. She's divine.

CONROY'S VOICE. Would you fuck her?

ED. Um.

CONROY'S VOICE. Have you fucked her?

ED. No.

CONROY'S VOICE. I found a condom with your name and address on it.

ED. We made love.

CONROY *marches out.*

CONROY. What did you just say?

ED. The truth.

CONROY. Cecil kill one of them.

CECIL *wraps her yoyo around* ISABEL*'s neck, strangling her.*

ED. PLEASE STOP STOP I'LL DO ANYTHING STOP!

CONROY. Cecil, stop.

CECIL *stops.*

Tonight you'll board a cargo ship to the West Indies.

ED. What?

CONROY. You'll go to the West Indies.

ED. I can't.

CONROY. Then I'll kill them both.

ED. I can't leave.

> CONROY *takes off the sacks to reveal* ISABEL *and* LAURIE, *their mouths stuffed.*

CONROY. This is your flesh and blood we're talking about?

> ED *shakes his head.*

Okay ladies, any last words?

> CONROY *takes out the balls/handkerchiefs stuffed in their mouths.*

LAURIE. Ed!?

ED....

CONROY. Isabel and Laurie Jones. I bid you, adieu.

> Fire it up Sasha.

> SASHA *fires up the chainsaw.*

> SASHA *is about to cut open* LAURIE's *head.*

ED. STOP STOP I'LL GO STOP PUT ME ON THE BOAT PUT ME ON THE BOAT.

CONROY. Stop.

> SASHA *turns off the chainsaw.*

> Write this letter.

> CONROY *hands* ED *parchment and a quill.*

> 'Dear Family,

> ED *writes as* CONROY *dictates.*

I have boarded a cargo boat bound for the West Indies. It is stuffed to the brim with... plantation utensils. I may not return. There are all sorts of economic opportunities in that part of the world. I also hear the women are wonderful.

All my love,

Ed Jones.'

Sign.

CONROY *inspects the letter.*

ED. Now let them go.

CONROY. When you step on the boat I'll release them, but for now – they're insurance.

ED. You have me in custody!

CONROY. I'm not taking any chances.

ED. My family are all here – who's the letter for?

CONROY. The letter might find its way to the Queen.

ED. No!

CONROY. Yes.

ED. VICTORIA! VICTORIA! VICTORIA!

CONROY *slaps* ED.

CONROY. As a show of good faith I'll release one.

Choose.

ED....

CONROY. Quickly.

ED. Isabel release Isabel.

CONROY. FRED!

FRED *comes out of the shed, dressed as a gimp.*

Escort Isabel out of Buckingham Palace.

FRED *puts a hessian sack over* ISABEL*'s head. His movement is slow and sultry. Then he uickly whips out a pistol and shoots* ISABEL *at point-blank range.* FRED *carries* ISABEL*'s lifeless body out.*

LAURIE *goes to scream but no sound comes out.*

ED *goes very still.*

Boat leaves at nine. Not long now.

Long pause.

SASHA. Lord Conroy would you like a sandwich?

CONROY. What's in it?

SASHA. Cheddar with a dash of pickle.

CONROY. Go on then.

SASHA *and* CONROY *eat sandwiches.*

ED *sings 'I Need to See You'.*

ED (*singing*).
  Vic open your eyes.
  I'm where you'd rather not see,
  Take your head out of the clouds.
  Come down and rescue me.

  If this was just a story, filled with made-up monsters,
  We'd dress up as heroes, fight the villains and win.
  Save my little sister, save her from this creature,
  Stop the world moving, hold me in your arms.

  I need to see you.
  You need to see me.
  Before fear blinds us both.
  I need to see you,
  You need to see me.

  All this rage inside
  Nowhere for it to go.
  Don't want a sponge.
  Just someone to help me grow.

  If this was just a story, filled with made-up monsters,
  We'd dress up as heroes, fight the villains and win.
  Save my little sister, save her from this creature,
  Stop the world moving, hold me in your arms.

I need to see you.
You need to see me.
Before fear blinds us both.
I need to see you,
You need to see me.

The DUCHESS *enters.*

DUCHESS. John, what's going on?

CONROY. What are you doing here?

DUCHESS. I heard screams.

CONROY. They're terrorists.

DUCHESS. They look like children.

CONROY. Terrorists come in all shapes and sizes.

DUCHESS. Has Victoria sanctioned this?

CONROY. Yes.

DUCHESS....

CONROY. My love, they are enemies of the state.

Beat.

DUCHESS *exits.*

Darling?

Shit.

Sasha go make her an omelette.

SASHA *exits.*

ED *and* LAURIE *look at each other. It's now two against two.*

LAURIE. What tricks can you do?

CECIL. Name a trick and I'll do it.

LAURIE. Cat's cradle.

CECIL. Schoolboy.

CECIL *does a cat's cradle. Looks at* LAURIE, *smug.*

LAURIE. What's the trick that no one else can do in the world?

CECIL *performs a trick/yoyo dance. It is astonishing.*

LAURIE *looks at* ED.

ED *jumps up and uses his handcuffs to make a noose around* CONROY*'s neck, strangling him.* LAURIE *picks up the chainsaw and drives it into* CONROY.

CECIL *stops her trick. Thinks about defending her boss. Decides to run away.*

CONROY (*to audience*). Basically Laurie is plunging the chainsaw into my chest.

CONROY *screams.* LAURIE *hacks.*

Okay basically she has removed both my arms, and has now made an incision at the waist, and is proceeding to cut me in half.

CONROY *screams.* LAURIE *cuts.*

Now just imagine my soul departing my mangled body and flying up to heaven, oh no there's a diversion and the soul is plummeting down to h–

CONROY *dies.*

ED *and* LAURIE *are covered in blood.*

VICTORIA *enters with the* DUCHESS, GARY *and* GUARDS.

DUCHESS. John…

Beat.

VICTORIA (*to* GARY). Take Mum to my room.

Everyone exits, leaving only VICTORIA, ED *and* LAURIE.

ED. This is my sister Laurie. Laurie this is –

LAURIE. I know who it is.

VICTORIA (*re:* CONROY). Was that necessary?

ED. He killed our sister.

LAURIE (*to* ED). Wait, you know her!?

ED....

LAURIE. You fucking coward you could have changed the world by now.

VICTORIA. What is she talking about?

LAURIE. It's not too late.

ED. Laurie stop.

LAURIE *hovers dangerously close to the chainsaw.*

A tense beat.

LAURIE *sits on the ground.*

LAURIE. Isabel...

LAURIE *tries to stop the tears.*

Pause.

VICTORIA *approaches to comfort.*

Don't touch me.

Beat.

Are you going to arrest us?

VICTORIA *shakes her head.*

Come on Ed. Let's go home.

ED. I'll catch up.

LAURIE....

Beat.

Can I have your autograph?

ED. Are you joking!?

LAURIE. Might as well make a bit of coin from all this.

VICTORIA. I'm not going to sign something for you to sell.

LAURIE. Why not?

VICTORIA....

Hand me that paper.

LAURIE *picks up the paper.*

VICTORIA *writes a note to* LAURIE.

LAURIE *looks at it.*

LAURIE (*desperate*). Ed. Come home tonight.

ED *nods.*

LAURIE *exits.*

VICTORIA *and* ED *take each other in.*

VICTORIA. I'm so sorry about your sister.

ED *bottles up his guilt and grief.*

ED. Your man Conroy was about to put me on a boat to the West Indies.

VICTORIA. Would that have been so terrible?

ED....

I've never done a long-distance relationship but can't imagine they're easy.

Beat.

VICTORIA. Albert's upstairs.

ED. Why?

VICTORIA. We're going to get married.

Pause.

ED. He's your cousin. It's...

VICTORIA. What?

ED. Medieval.

VICTORIA. That would be marrying a brother.

ED. Cousins, brothers, it's all the same.

VICTORIA. Most civilised people marry their cousins.

ED. You'll probably have stupid children. When you fuck a family member there's too much shared stuff to spark anything original.

Beat.

VICTORIA. I love him.

ED. Course you do he's your cousin.

VICTORIA. More than that.

ED. How!?

VICTORIA. He's thoughtful caring sensitive intelligent musical kind sweet-natured.

ED. Sounds like you're trying to persuade yourself.

VICTORIA. He's loving!

ED. In what way!?

VICTORIA. He makes me feel… unearthly.

Beat.

ED. Bollocks.

VICTORIA. He knows who he is.

ED. That is so… you are so… predictable.

Upstairs is he? I'll kill him.

VICTORIA. Then I'll have you hanged.

ED. This whole thing is a… charade.

VICTORIA. It's not a charade. It's a… love story.

ED. A love story?

ED *picks up the chainsaw.*

The most dangerous beat.

VICTORIA. I think you should go to New York.

> ED *puts down the chainsaw.*

> Think of it as a fresh start.

ED. Why are you being so cruel?

VICTORIA. Don't you wanna grow up?

> *Beat.*

> I actually think New York is a really good idea. Set you free from the monotony of your life.

ED. I'm okay with my life.

VICTORIA. In and out of prison?

ED. The bits in between sweeten the deal.

VICTORIA. I'm sending you to New York.

ED. I can't leave Laurie.

VICTORIA. Take her with, I'll arrange it.

ED. Don't you dare.

VICTORIA. Then where else would you like to go?

ED. You might as well send me to Australia.

VICTORIA. Okay then.

ED. What!?

> *Faintly we hear 'The Best Things in Life are Free'.*

VICTORIA. You're in Australia.

ED. Am I?

VICTORIA. A journalist down under. You edit the national paper. It's committed to serious ideas not just rumours.

ED. I love rumours!

VICTORIA. At night you chill on the beach, look up at the stars, and drink beer.

ED. Yeah I'm tanked up. I'm so drunk I think I can fly, but of course I can't. So I decide to swim.

VICTORIA. Don't do that you'll drown.

ED. Too late I've just swum past South Africa.

VICTORIA. Turn back, the sharks will get at you.

ED. Sharks? As if. I'm Boy Jones.

VICTORIA. Speak in third person now?

ED. Yeah becoming famous. It's fucking changed me.

VICTORIA. Uh-oh you're drowning.

ED. Bollocks I'm doing butterfly past Morocco.

VICTORIA. You're tangled up in some rubbish.

ED. Past Spain, Portugal, France.

VICTORIA. Now you're suffocating.

ED. I can see the cliffs! I can see the white cliffs!

VICTORIA *runs at* ED *run very fast at each other and stop. Their noses almost touching.*

Their breath falls into sync.

The lights fade.

All we can hear is their breath.

The End.